SPYING FOR FREEDOM

JAMES LAFAYETTE'S STORY

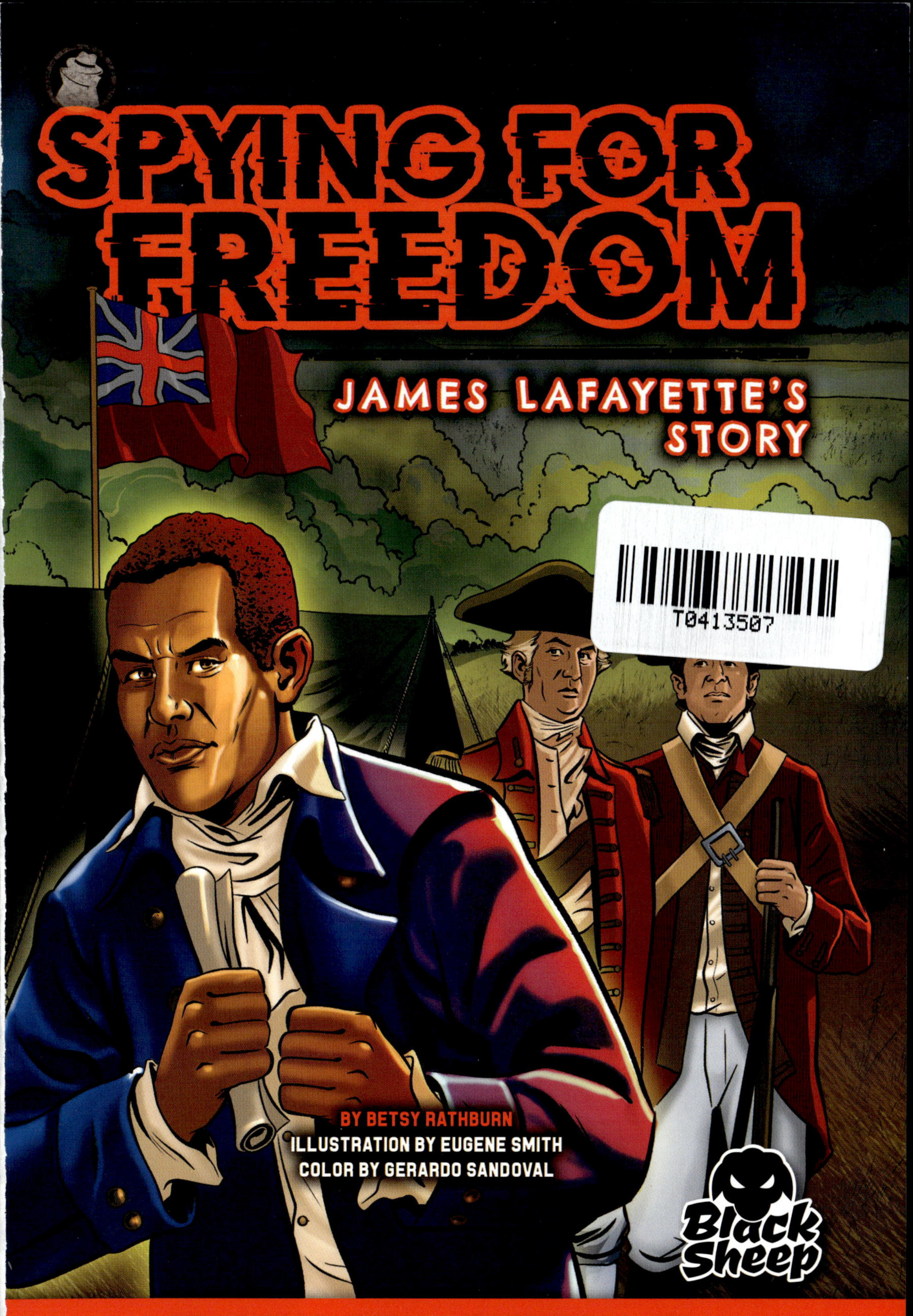

BY BETSY RATHBURN
ILLUSTRATION BY EUGENE SMITH
COLOR BY GERARDO SANDOVAL

Black Sheep

BELLWETHER MEDIA • MINNEAPOLIS, MN

Stray from regular reads with Black Sheep books. Feel a rush with every read!

This edition first published in 2025 by Bellwether Media, Inc.

No part of this publication may be reproduced in whole or in part without written permission of the publisher. For information regarding permission, write to Bellwether Media, Inc., Attention: Permissions Department, 6012 Blue Circle Drive, Minnetonka, MN 55343.

Library of Congress Cataloging-in-Publication Data

Names: Rathburn, Betsy, author. | Smith, Eugene (Illustrator), illustrator.
Title: Spying for freedom : James Lafayette's story / by Betsy Rathburn ; illustrated by] Eugene Smith.
Description: Minneapolis, MN : Bellwether Media, Inc., 2025. | Series: Black Sheep : Top secret spy stories | Includes bibliographical references and index. | Audience: Ages 7-13 | Audience: Grades 4-6 | Summary: "Exciting illustrations follow the events of James Lafayette's spying career. The combination of brightly colored panels and leveled text is intended for students in grades 3 through 8"– Provided by publisher.
Identifiers: LCCN 2024021932 (print) | LCCN 2024021933 (ebook) | ISBN 9798893040586 (library binding) | ISBN 9798893041651 (paperback) | ISBN 9781648348921 (ebook)
Subjects: LCSH: Lafayette, James Armistead, 1760?-1830–Juvenile literature. | United States–History–Revolution, 1775-1783–Secret service–Juvenile literature. | Spies–United States–Biography–Juvenile literature. | United States –History–Revolution, 1775-1783–African Americans–Biography–Juvenile literature. | Lafayette, James Armistead, 1760?-1830–Comic books, strips, etc. | United States–History–Revolution, 1775-1783–Secret service–Comic books, strips, etc. | Spies–United States–Biography–Comic books, strips, etc. | United States–History–Revolution, 1775-1783–African Americans–Biography–Comic books, strips, etc.
Classification: LCC E280.L34 R38 2025 (print) | LCC E280.L34 (ebook) | DDC 973.3/85092 [B]–dc23/eng/20240514
LC record available at https://lccn.loc.gov/2024021932
LC ebook record available at https://lccn.loc.gov/2024021933

Text copyright © 2025 by Bellwether Media, Inc. BLACK SHEEP and associated logos are trademarks and/or registered trademarks of Bellwether Media, Inc. Bellwether Media is a division of Chrysalis Education Group.

Editor: Christina Leaf   Designer: Andrea Schneider

Printed in the United States of America, North Mankato, MN.

TABLE OF CONTENTS

BECOMING A SPY..............4
SPY LIFE......................8
INDEPENDENCE.............16
   AND FREEDOM
MORE ABOUT................22
   JAMES LAFAYETTE
GLOSSARY...................23
TO LEARN MORE............24
INDEX........................24

Red text identifies historical quotes.

BECOMING A SPY

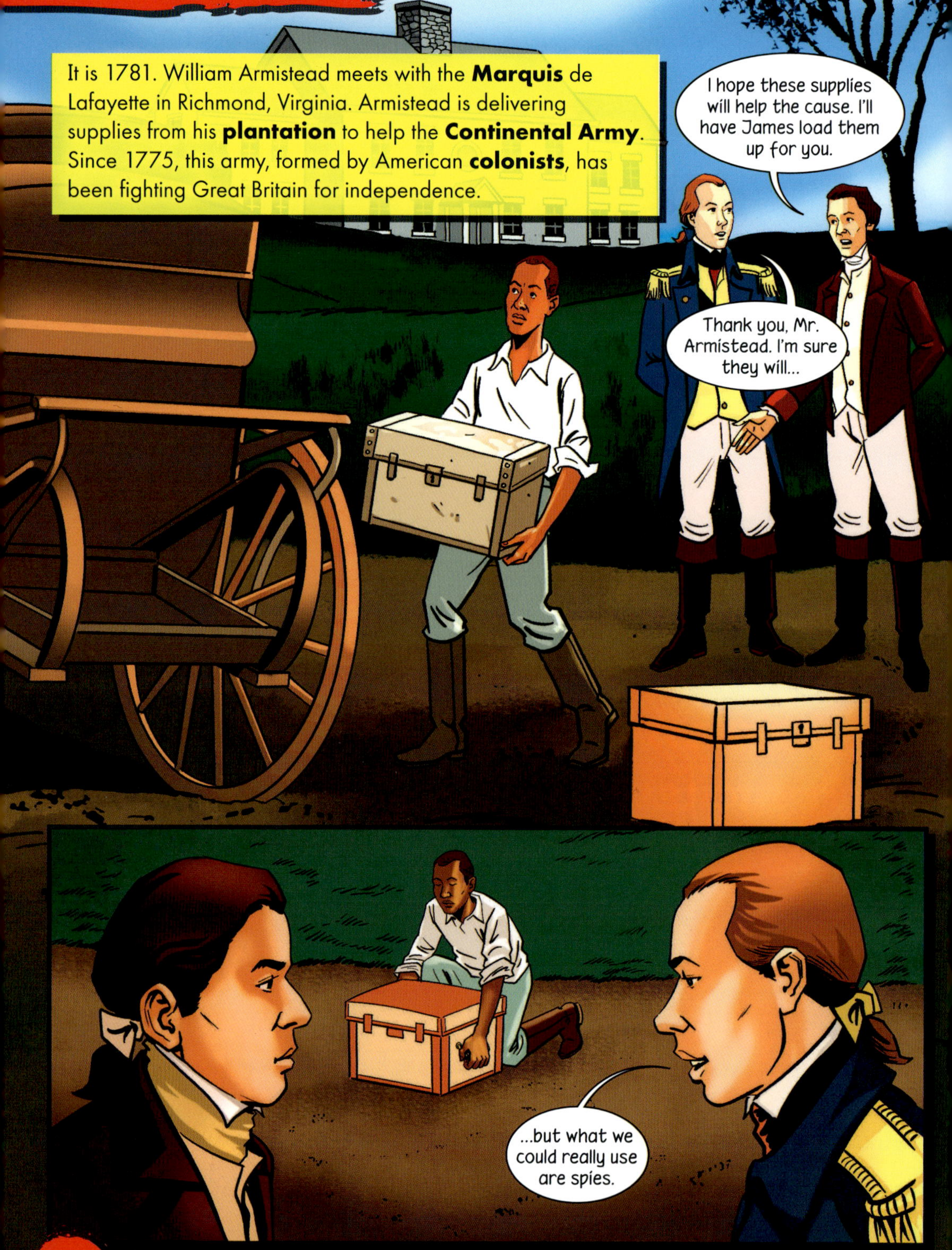
It is 1781. William Armistead meets with the **Marquis** de Lafayette in Richmond, Virginia. Armistead is delivering supplies from his **plantation** to help the **Continental Army**. Since 1775, this army, formed by American **colonists**, has been fighting Great Britain for independence.
I hope these supplies will help the cause. I'll have James load them up for you.
Thank you, Mr. Armistead. I'm sure they will...
...but what we could really use are spies.

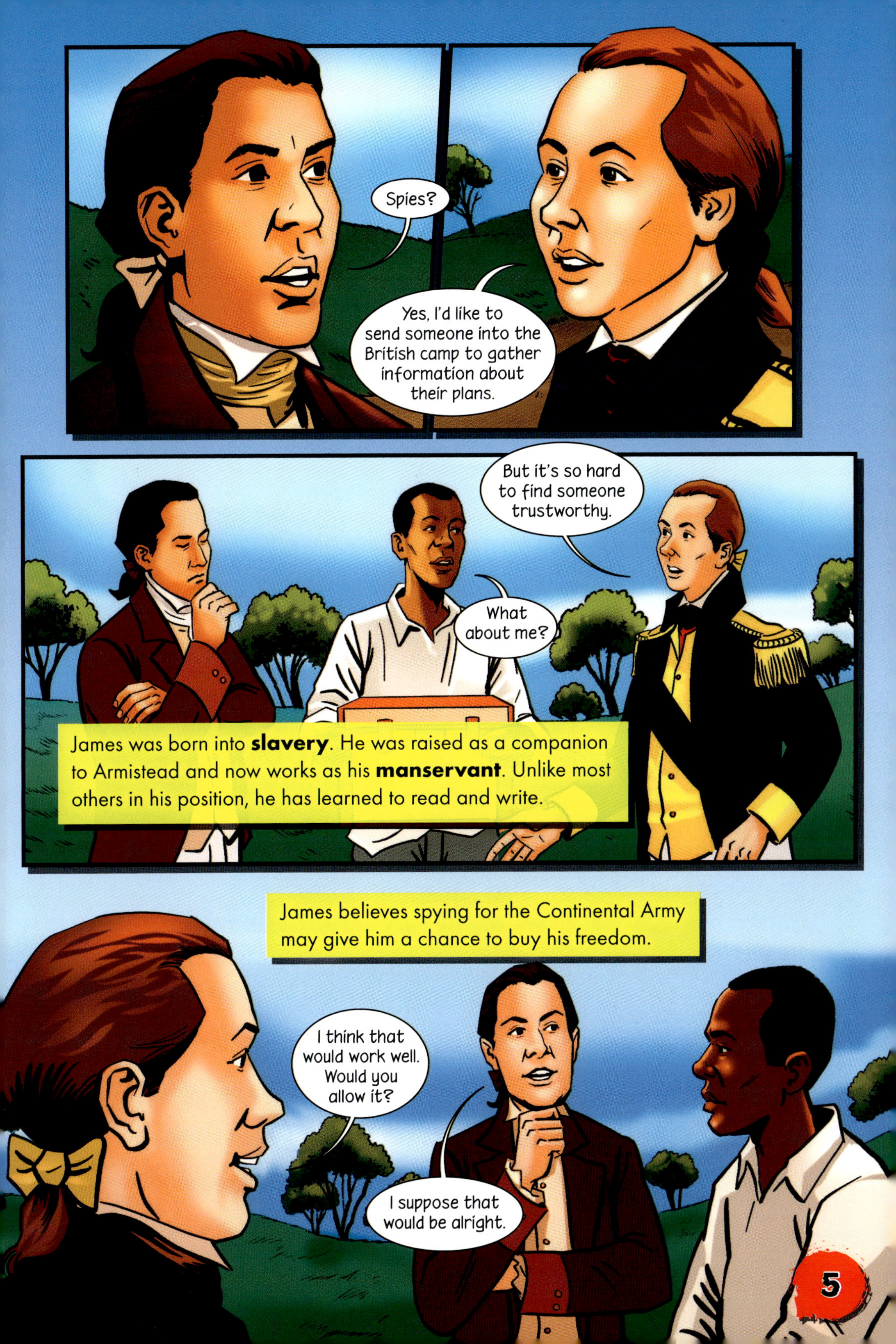
Spies?
Yes, I'd like to send someone into the British camp to gather information about their plans.
But it's so hard to find someone trustworthy.
What about me?
James was born into **slavery**. He was raised as a companion to Armistead and now works as his **manservant**. Unlike most others in his position, he has learned to read and write.
James believes spying for the Continental Army may give him a chance to buy his freedom.
I think that would work well. Would you allow it?
I suppose that would be alright.

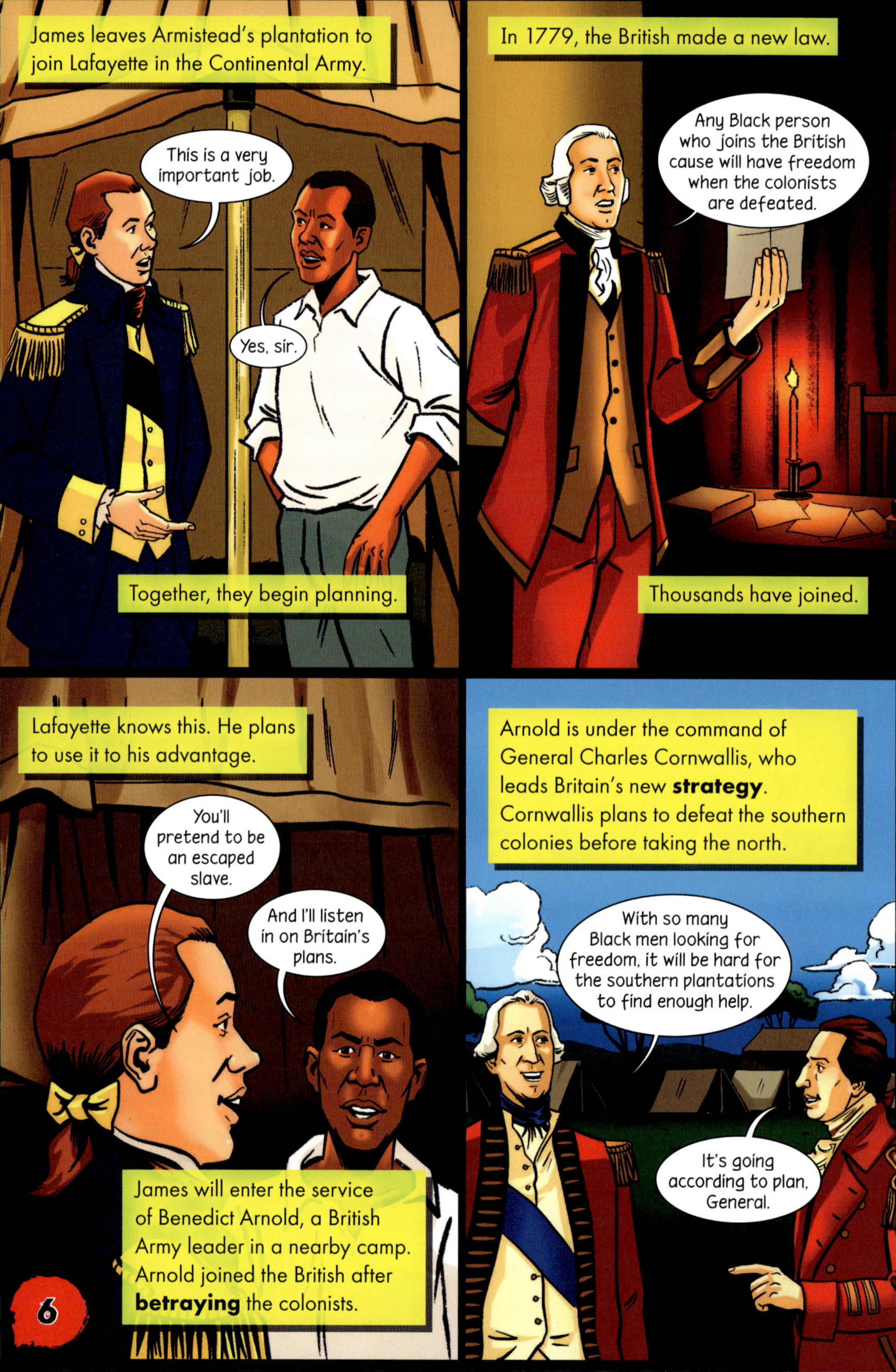
James leaves Armistead's plantation to join Lafayette in the Continental Army.
This is a very important job.
Yes, sir.
Together, they begin planning.
In 1779, the British made a new law.
Any Black person who joins the British cause will have freedom when the colonists are defeated.
Thousands have joined.
Lafayette knows this. He plans to use it to his advantage.
You'll pretend to be an escaped slave.
And I'll listen in on Britain's plans.
James will enter the service of Benedict Arnold, a British Army leader in a nearby camp. Arnold joined the British after **betraying** the colonists.
Arnold is under the command of General Charles Cornwallis, who leads Britain's new **strategy**. Cornwallis plans to defeat the southern colonies before taking the north.
With so many Black men looking for freedom, it will be hard for the southern plantations to find enough help.
It's going according to plan, General.

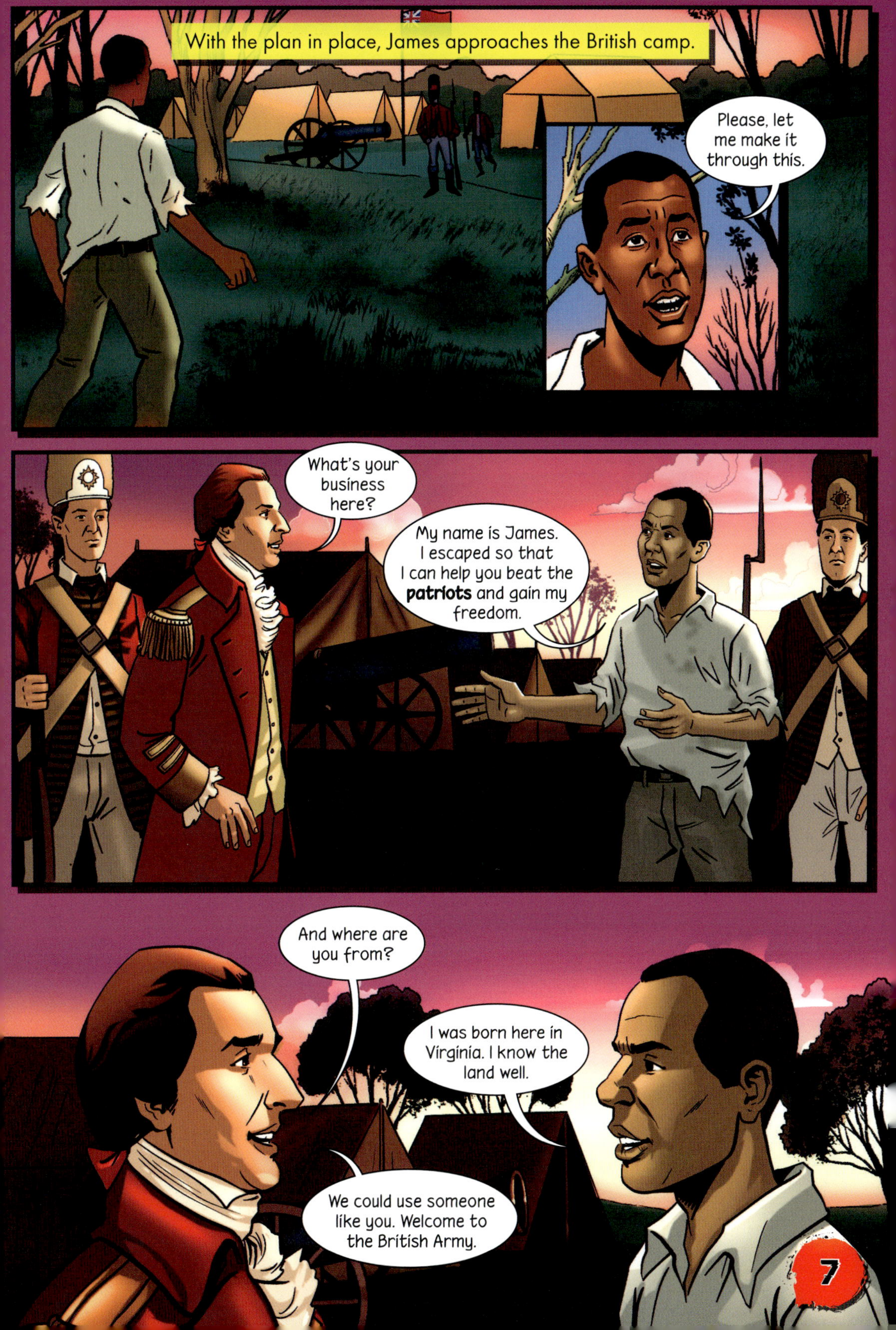

With the plan in place, James approaches the British camp.
Please, let me make it through this.
What's your business here?
My name is James. I escaped so that I can help you beat the **patriots** and gain my freedom.
And where are you from?
I was born here in Virginia. I know the land well.
We could use someone like you. Welcome to the British Army.

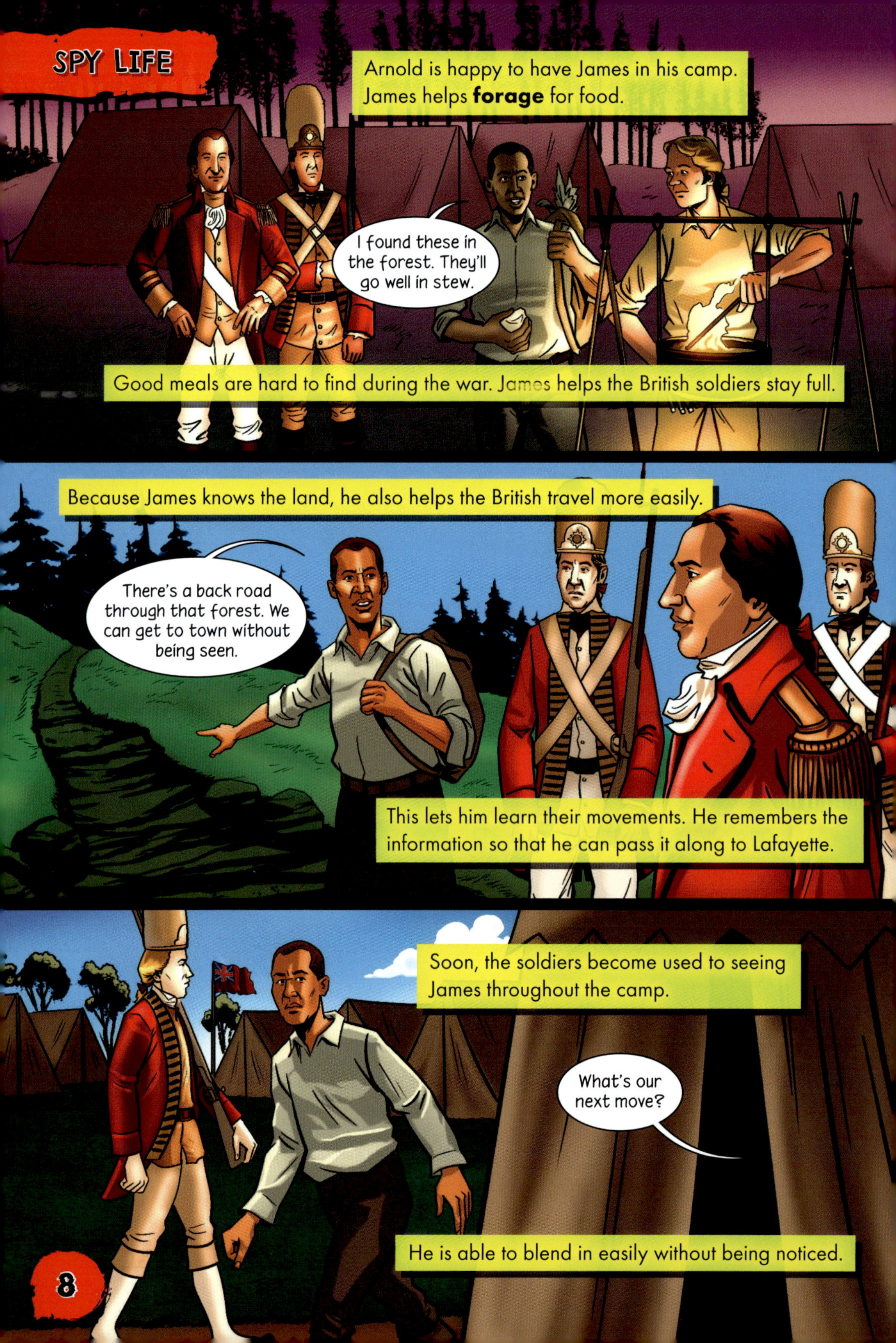
Arnold is happy to have James in his camp. James helps **forage** for food.
I found these in the forest. They'll go well in stew.
Good meals are hard to find during the war. James helps the British soldiers stay full.
Because James knows the land, he also helps the British travel more easily.
There's a back road through that forest. We can get to town without being seen.
This lets him learn their movements. He remembers the information so that he can pass it along to Lafayette.
Soon, the soldiers become used to seeing James throughout the camp.
What's our next move?
He is able to blend in easily without being noticed.

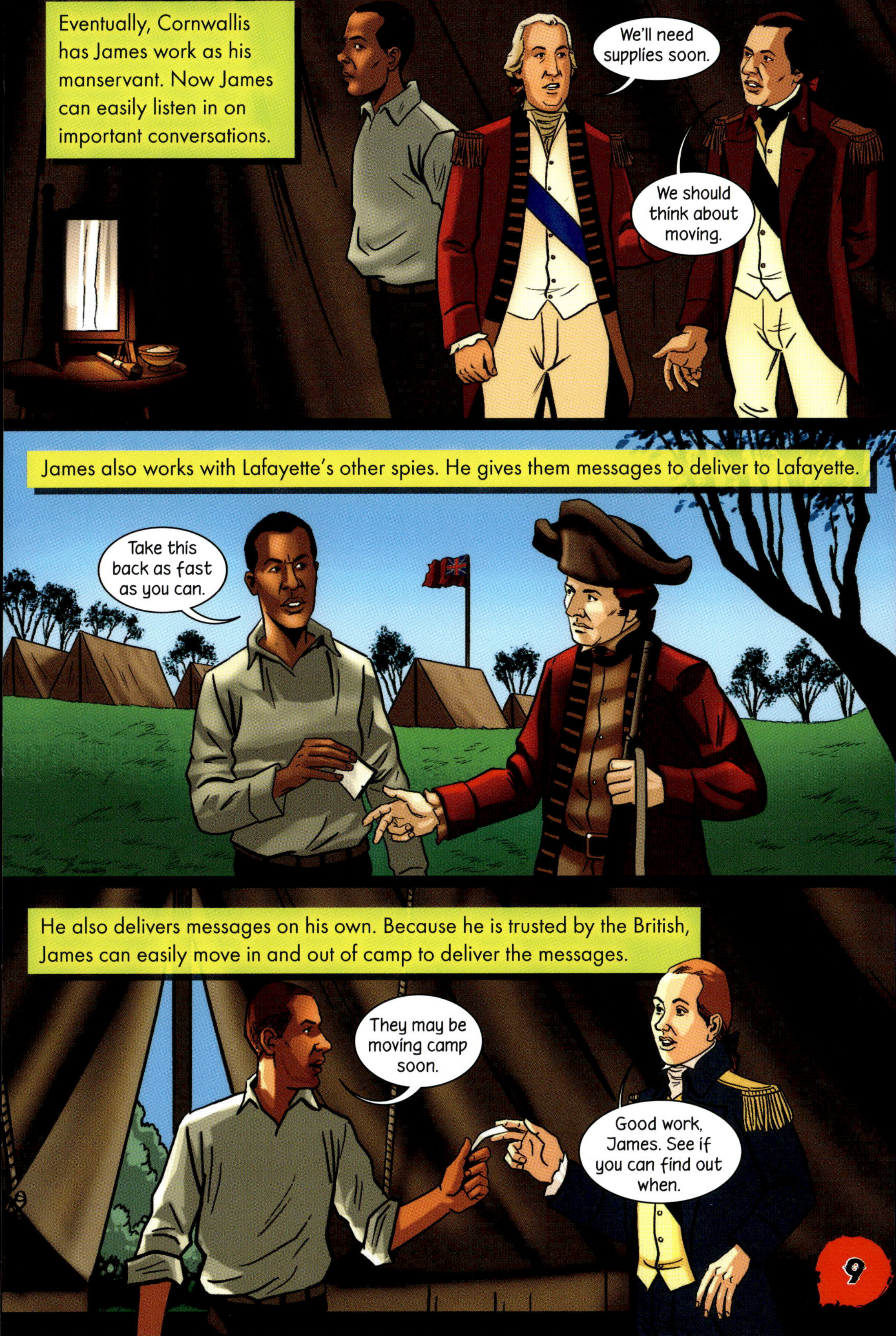
Eventually, Cornwallis has James work as his manservant. Now James can easily listen in on important conversations.
We'll need supplies soon.
We should think about moving.
James also works with Lafayette's other spies. He gives them messages to deliver to Lafayette.
Take this back as fast as you can.
He also delivers messages on his own. Because he is trusted by the British, James can easily move in and out of camp to deliver the messages.
They may be moving camp soon.
Good work, James. See if you can find out when.

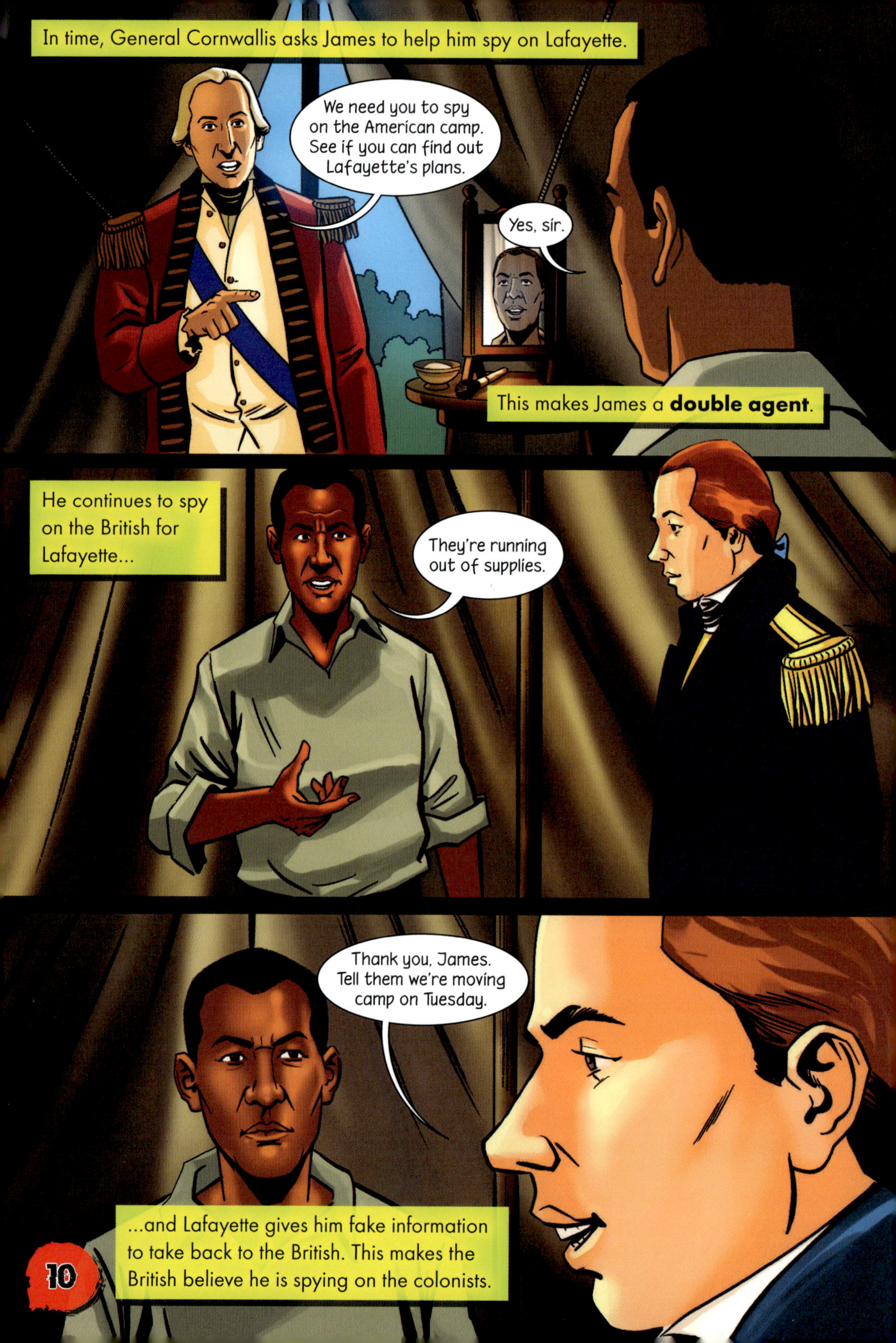
In time, General Cornwallis asks James to help him spy on Lafayette.
We need you to spy on the American camp. See if you can find out Lafayette's plans.
Yes, sir.
This makes James a **double agent**.
He continues to spy on the British for Lafayette...
They're running out of supplies.
Thank you, James. Tell them we're moving camp on Tuesday.
...and Lafayette gives him fake information to take back to the British. This makes the British believe he is spying on the colonists.

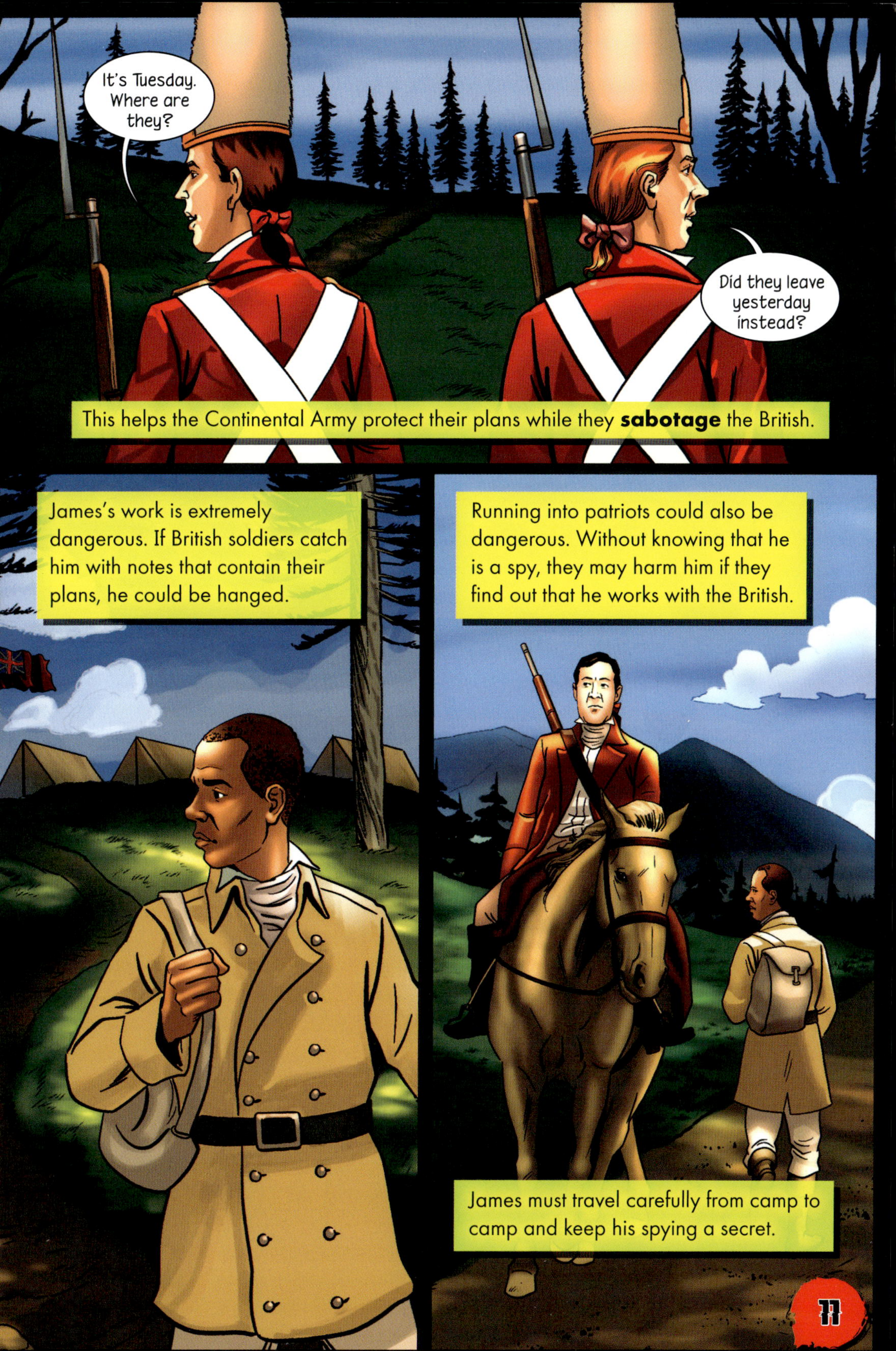
It's Tuesday. Where are they?
Did they leave yesterday instead?
This helps the Continental Army protect their plans while they **sabotage** the British.
James's work is extremely dangerous. If British soldiers catch him with notes that contain their plans, he could be hanged.
Running into patriots could also be dangerous. Without knowing that he is a spy, they may harm him if they find out that he works with the British.
James must travel carefully from camp to camp and keep his spying a secret.

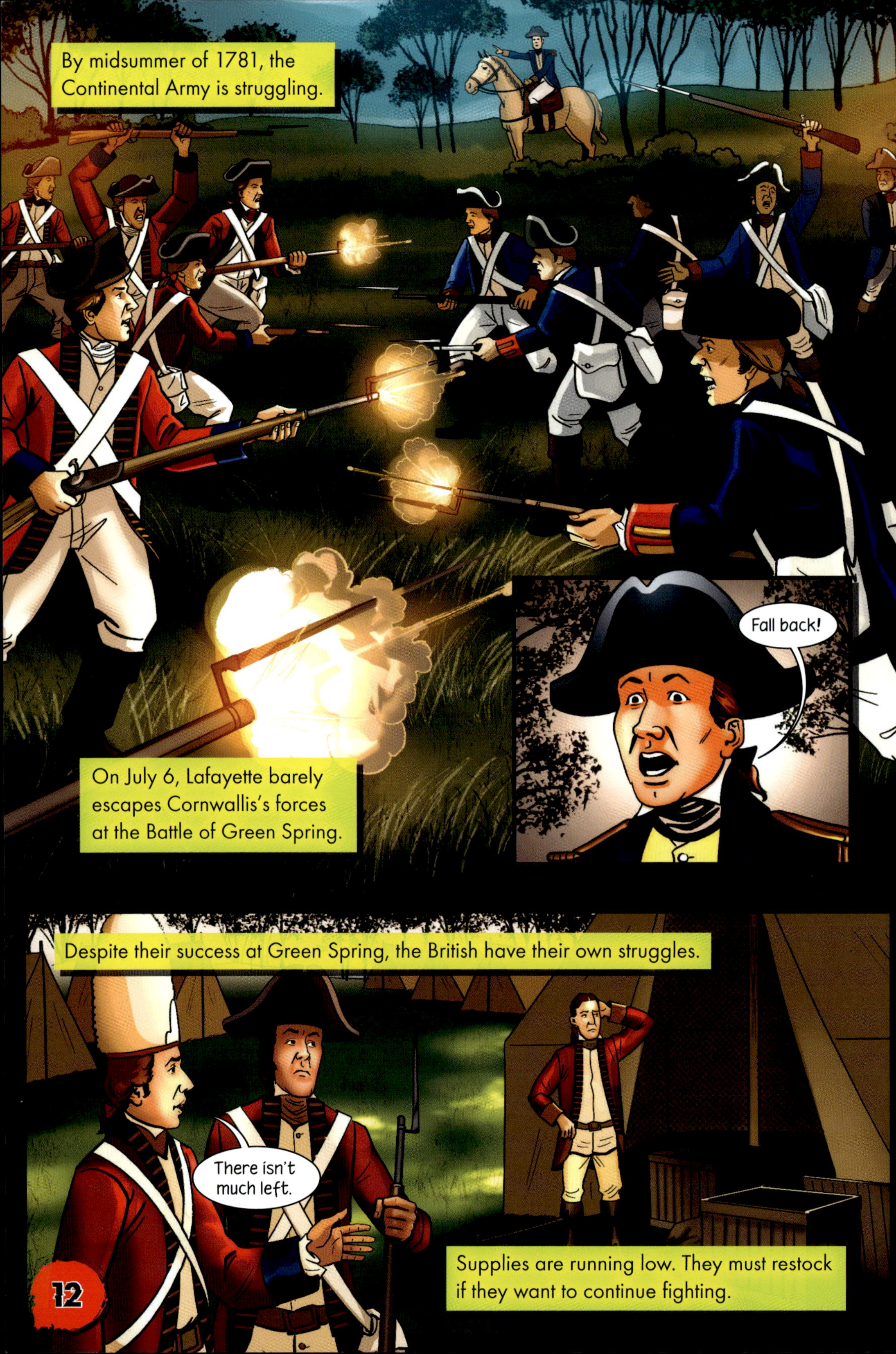
By midsummer of 1781, the Continental Army is struggling.
On July 6, Lafayette barely escapes Cornwallis's forces at the Battle of Green Spring.
Fall back!
Despite their success at Green Spring, the British have their own struggles.
There isn't much left.
Supplies are running low. They must restock if they want to continue fighting.

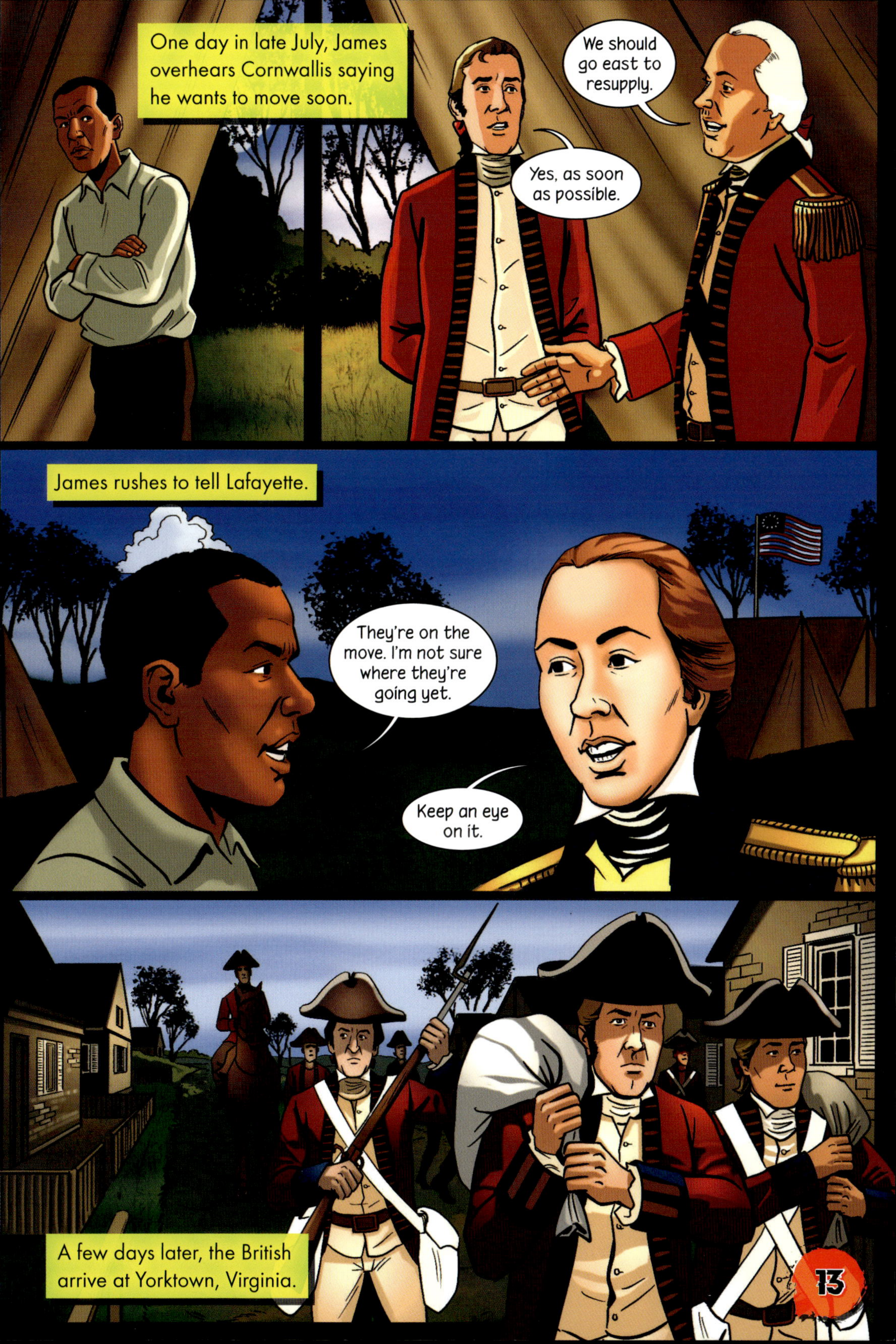

One day in late July, James overhears Cornwallis saying he wants to move soon.
We should go east to resupply.
Yes, as soon as possible.
James rushes to tell Lafayette.
They're on the move. I'm not sure where they're going yet.
Keep an eye on it.
A few days later, the British arrive at Yorktown, Virginia.

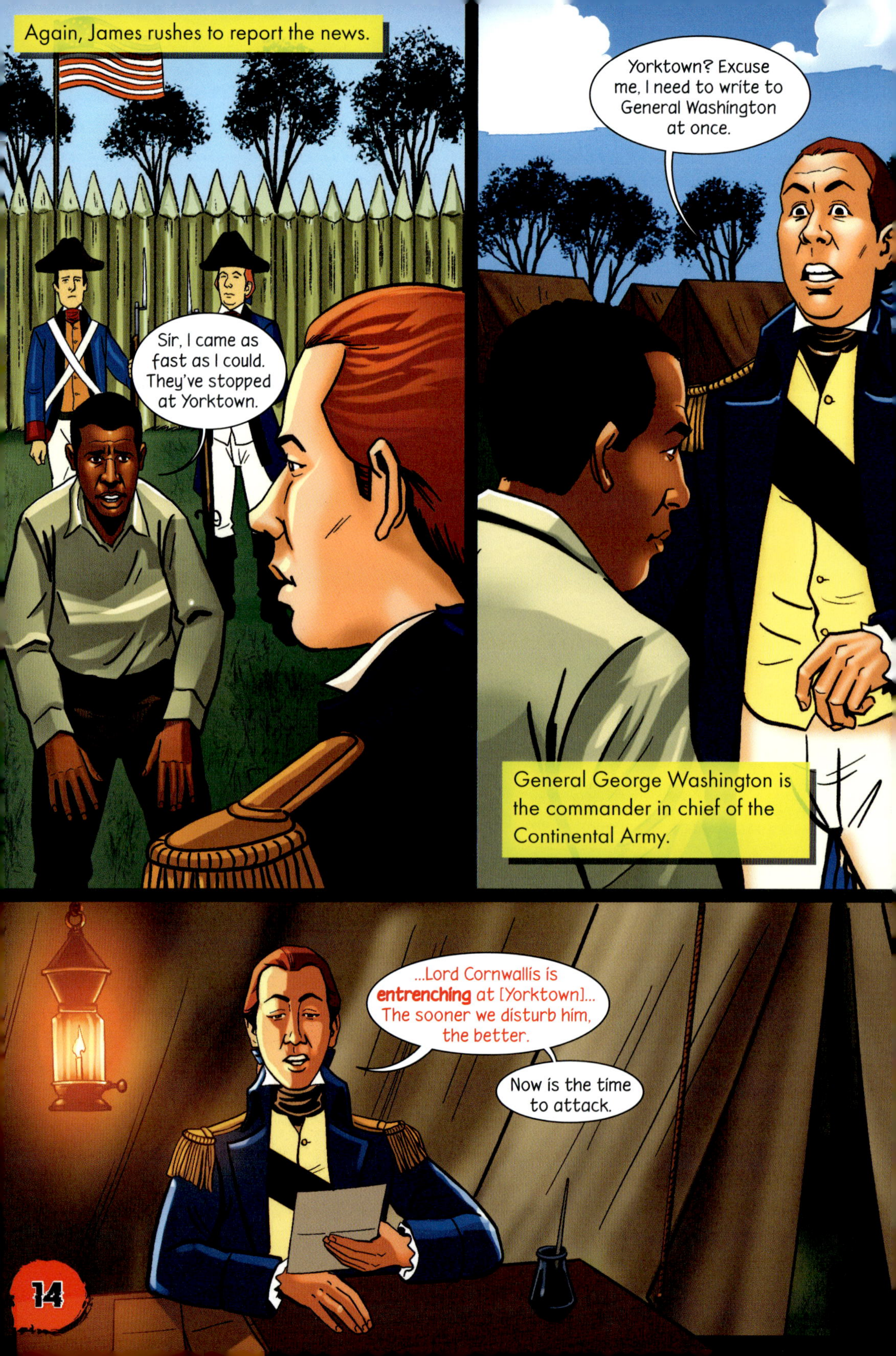

Again, James rushes to report the news.
Sir, I came as fast as I could. They've stopped at Yorktown.
Yorktown? Excuse me, I need to write to General Washington at once.
General George Washington is the commander in chief of the Continental Army.
...Lord Cornwallis is **entrenching** at [Yorktown]... The sooner we disturb him, the better.
Now is the time to attack.

Take this to General Washington as quickly as possible. And be careful. If this falls into the wrong hands...
You have my word.
Washington is in New York, hundreds of miles away. It will take two weeks to deliver the message.
By mid-August, Cornwallis has **fortified** at Yorktown. He awaits a ship that will deliver supplies and help him communicate with British commanders.
I hope they arrive soon.
Meanwhile, Washington has received his message from Lafayette. Around August 21, he leaves New York.
Along with 2,500 American soldiers and 4,000 French soldiers, he marches in secret toward Virginia.
At sea, French **admiral** Comte de Grasse sails with a **fleet** of 37 ships. He hopes to stop the British from aiding Cornwallis.
Thanks to James's spying and Lafayette's quick action, the last act of the Revolutionary War is about to begin.

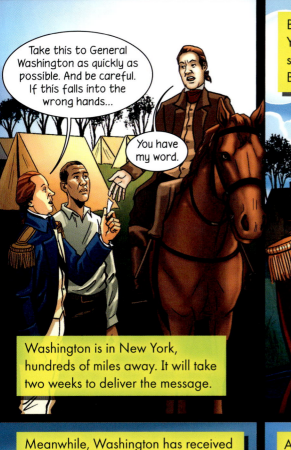

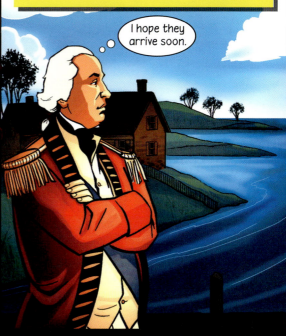

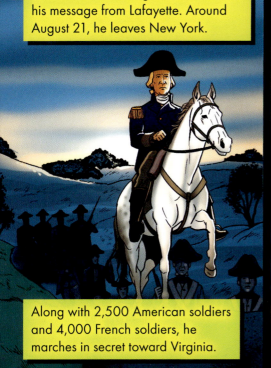

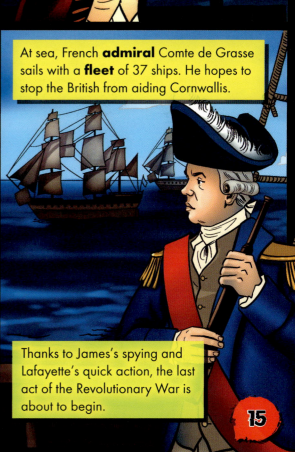

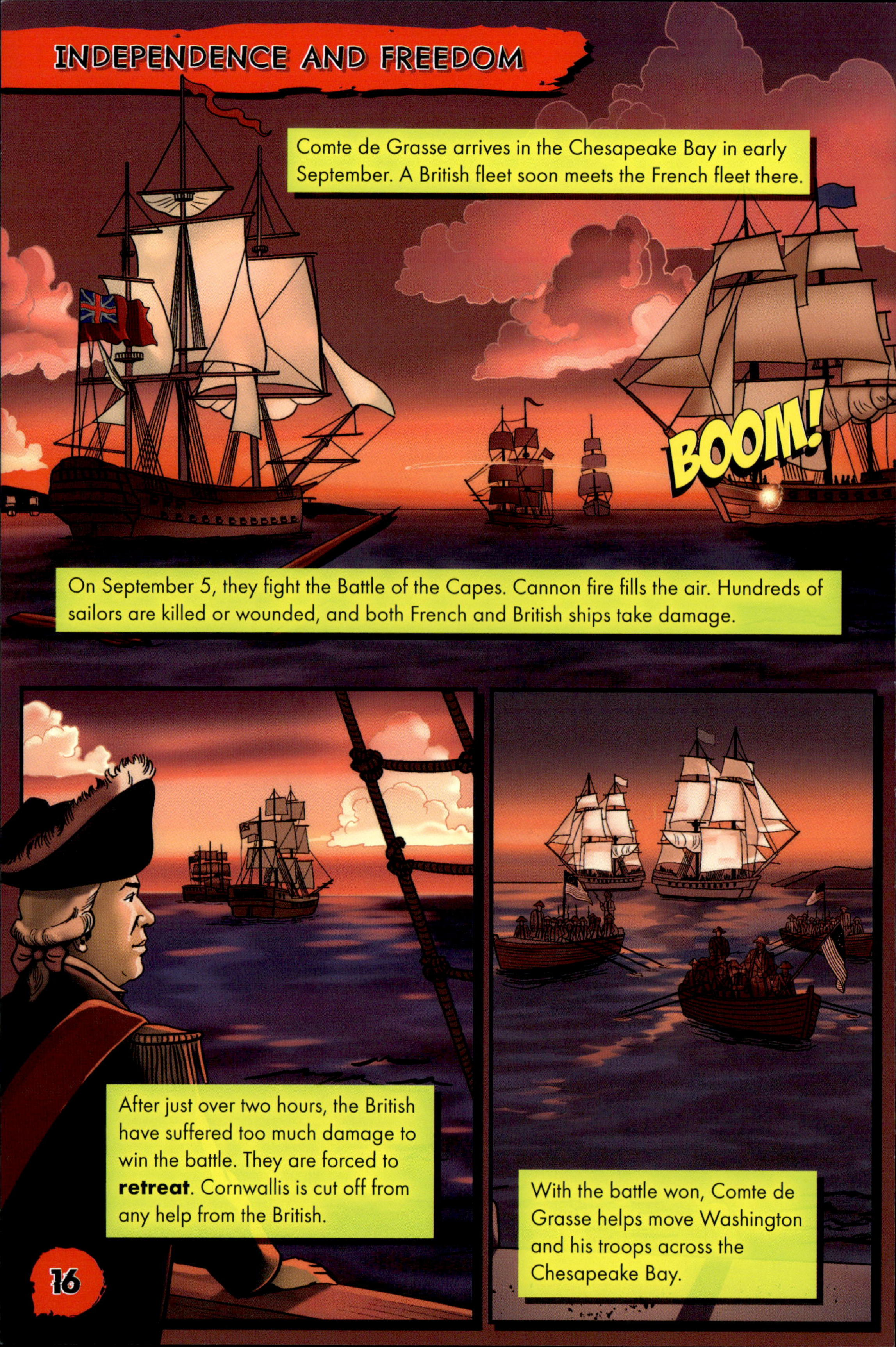
Comte de Grasse arrives in the Chesapeake Bay in early September. A British fleet soon meets the French fleet there.
BOOM!
On September 5, they fight the Battle of the Capes. Cannon fire fills the air. Hundreds of sailors are killed or wounded, and both French and British ships take damage.
After just over two hours, the British have suffered too much damage to win the battle. They are forced to **retreat**. Cornwallis is cut off from any help from the British.
With the battle won, Comte de Grasse helps move Washington and his troops across the Chesapeake Bay.

By mid-September, Washington and his troops have arrived in Williamsburg, Virginia. Washington meets with Lafayette to plan their next moves.
We're about 13 miles from Yorktown.
We should hurry and strike Cornwallis while we have the chance.
They dig a **trench** about half a mile from an area held by the British and prepare for battle.
On October 9, the Continental Army begins firing at the British. British fortifications are destroyed. Many soldiers are killed. Cornwallis's army begins to run out of supplies.
Finally, on October 19, General Cornwallis **surrenders**.
Cornwallis meets with Lafayette. He sees James among the Americans and finally understands that he has been lied to.
I never should have trusted you!
But it is too late now. The colonists' fight for independence is over!

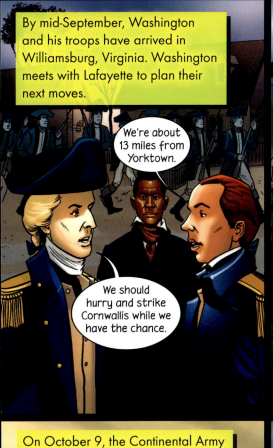

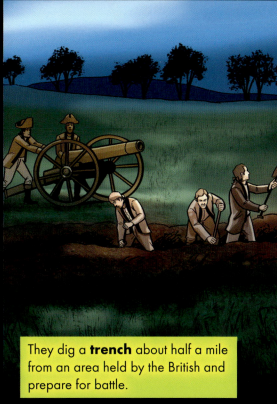

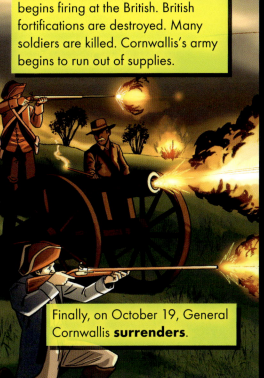

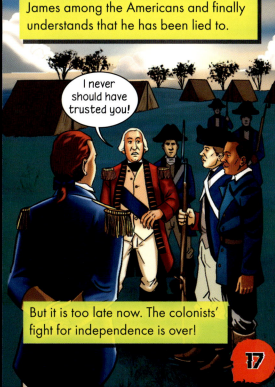

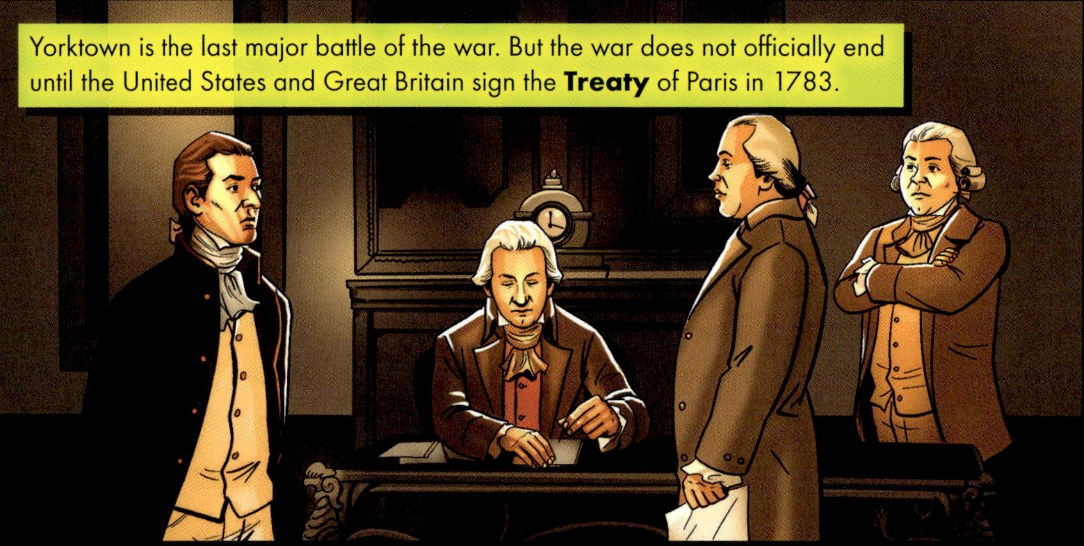
Yorktown is the last major battle of the war. But the war does not officially end until the United States and Great Britain sign the **Treaty** of Paris in 1783.

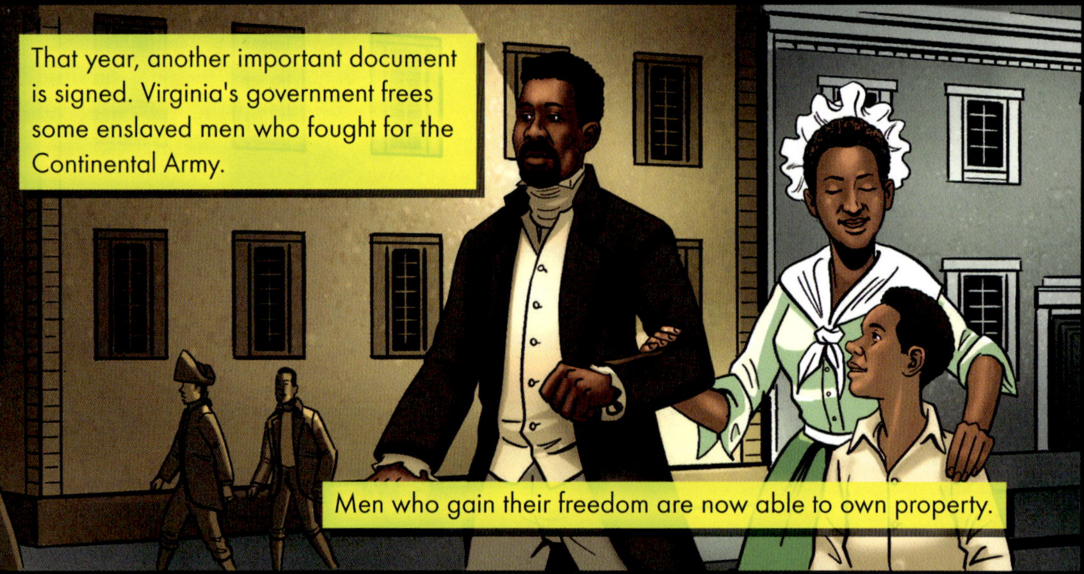
That year, another important document is signed. Virginia's government frees some enslaved men who fought for the Continental Army.
Men who gain their freedom are now able to own property.

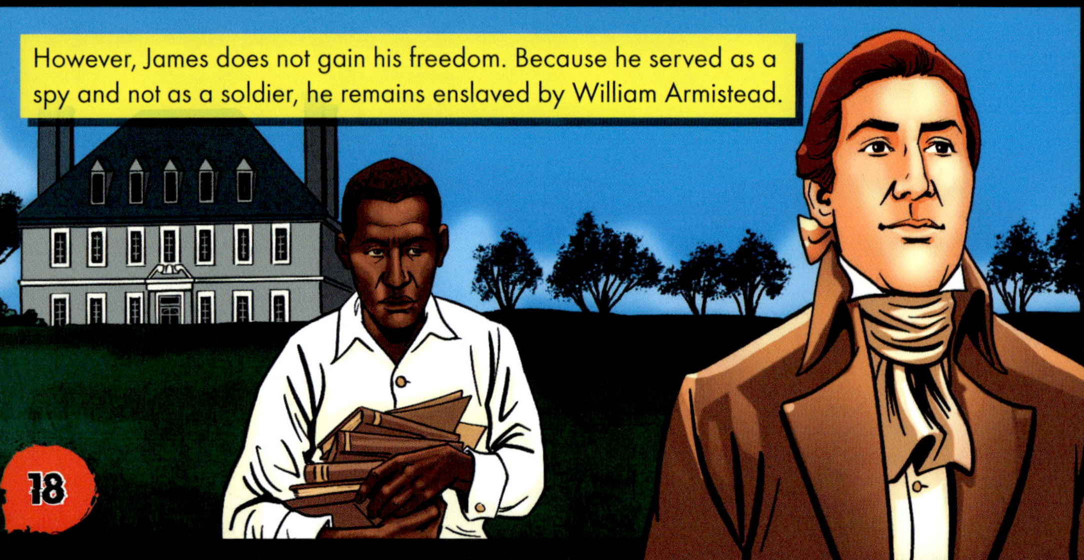
However, James does not gain his freedom. Because he served as a spy and not as a soldier, he remains enslaved by William Armistead.

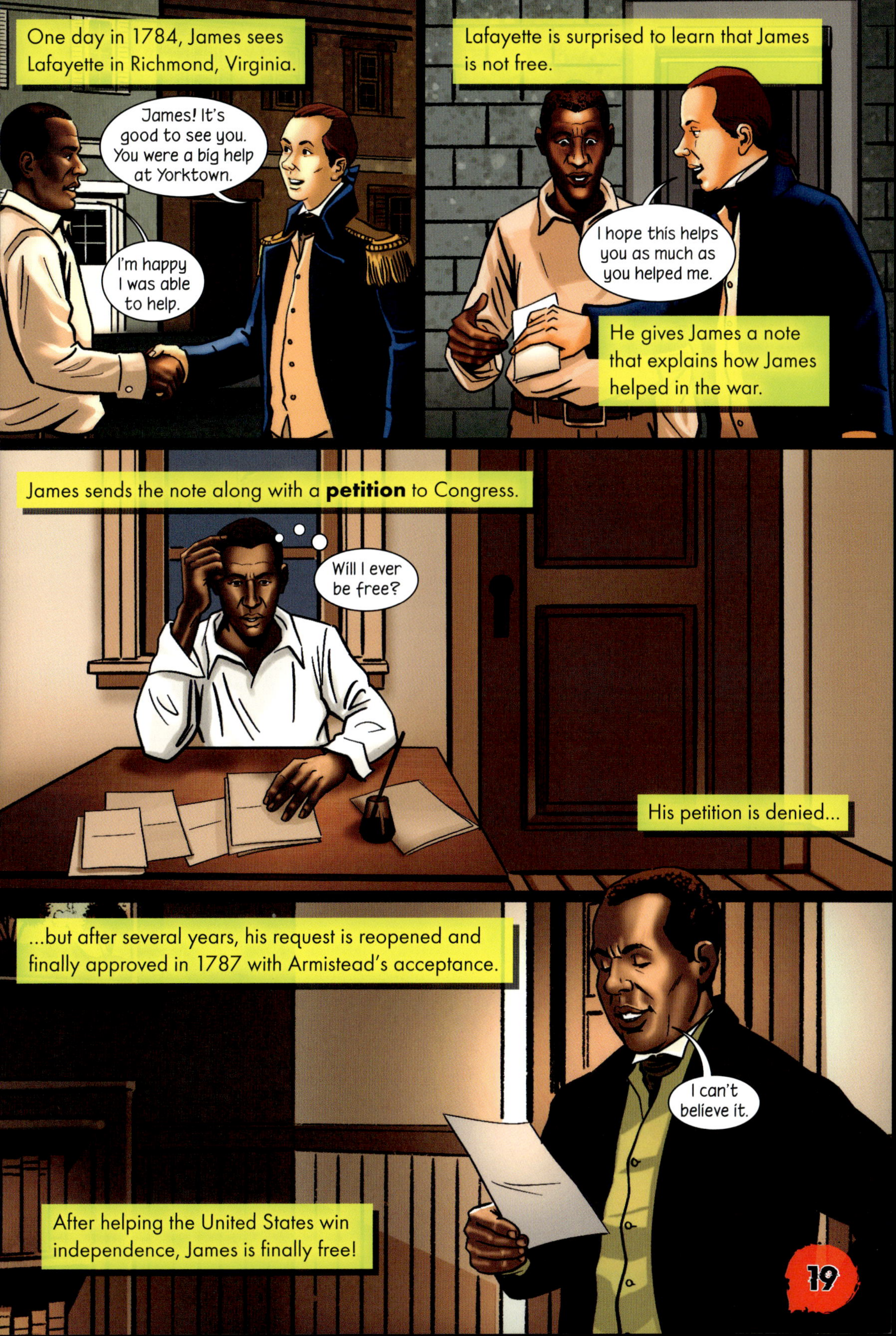

One day in 1784, James sees Lafayette in Richmond, Virginia.
James! It's good to see you. You were a big help at Yorktown.
I'm happy I was able to help.
Lafayette is surprised to learn that James is not free.
I hope this helps you as much as you helped me.
He gives James a note that explains how James helped in the war.
James sends the note along with a **petition** to Congress.
Will I ever be free?
His petition is denied...
...but after several years, his request is reopened and finally approved in 1787 with Armistead's acceptance.
I can't believe it.
After helping the United States win independence, James is finally free!

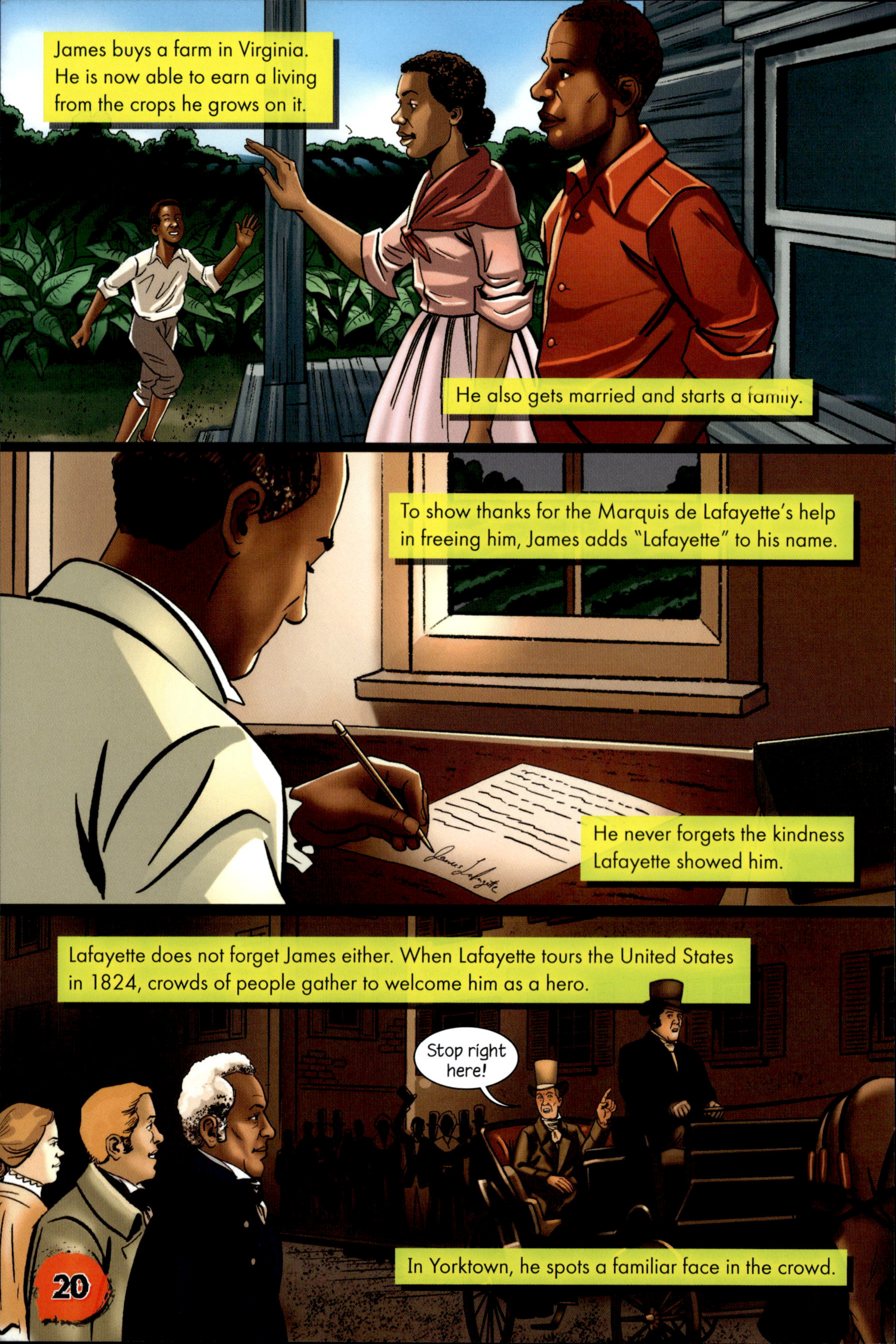
James buys a farm in Virginia. He is now able to earn a living from the crops he grows on it.
He also gets married and starts a family.
To show thanks for the Marquis de Lafayette's help in freeing him, James adds "Lafayette" to his name.
James Lafayette
He never forgets the kindness Lafayette showed him.
Lafayette does not forget James either. When Lafayette tours the United States in 1824, crowds of people gather to welcome him as a hero.
Stop right here!
In Yorktown, he spots a familiar face in the crowd.

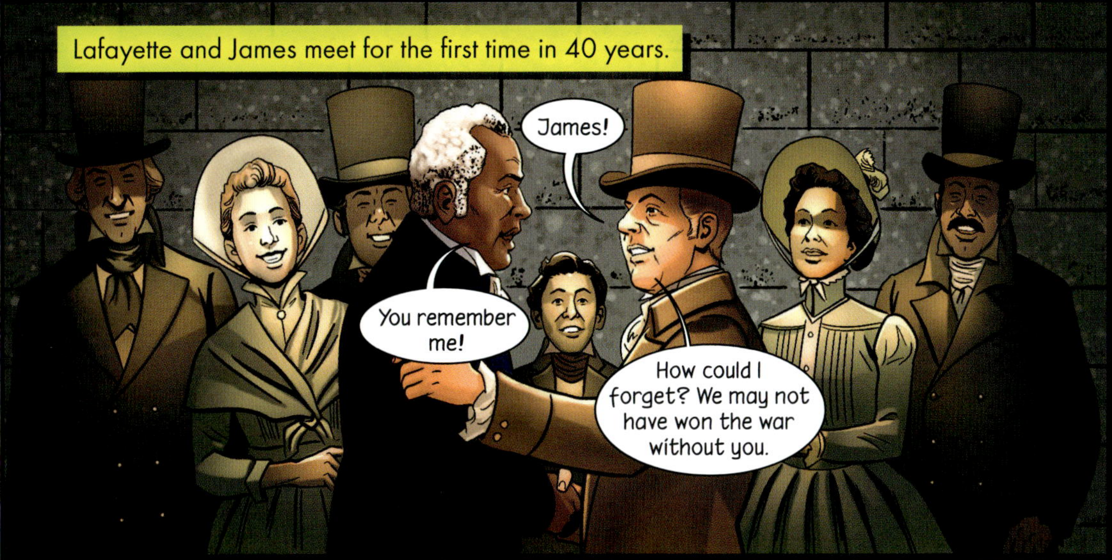
Lafayette and James meet for the first time in 40 years.
James!
You remember me!
How could I forget? We may not have won the war without you.

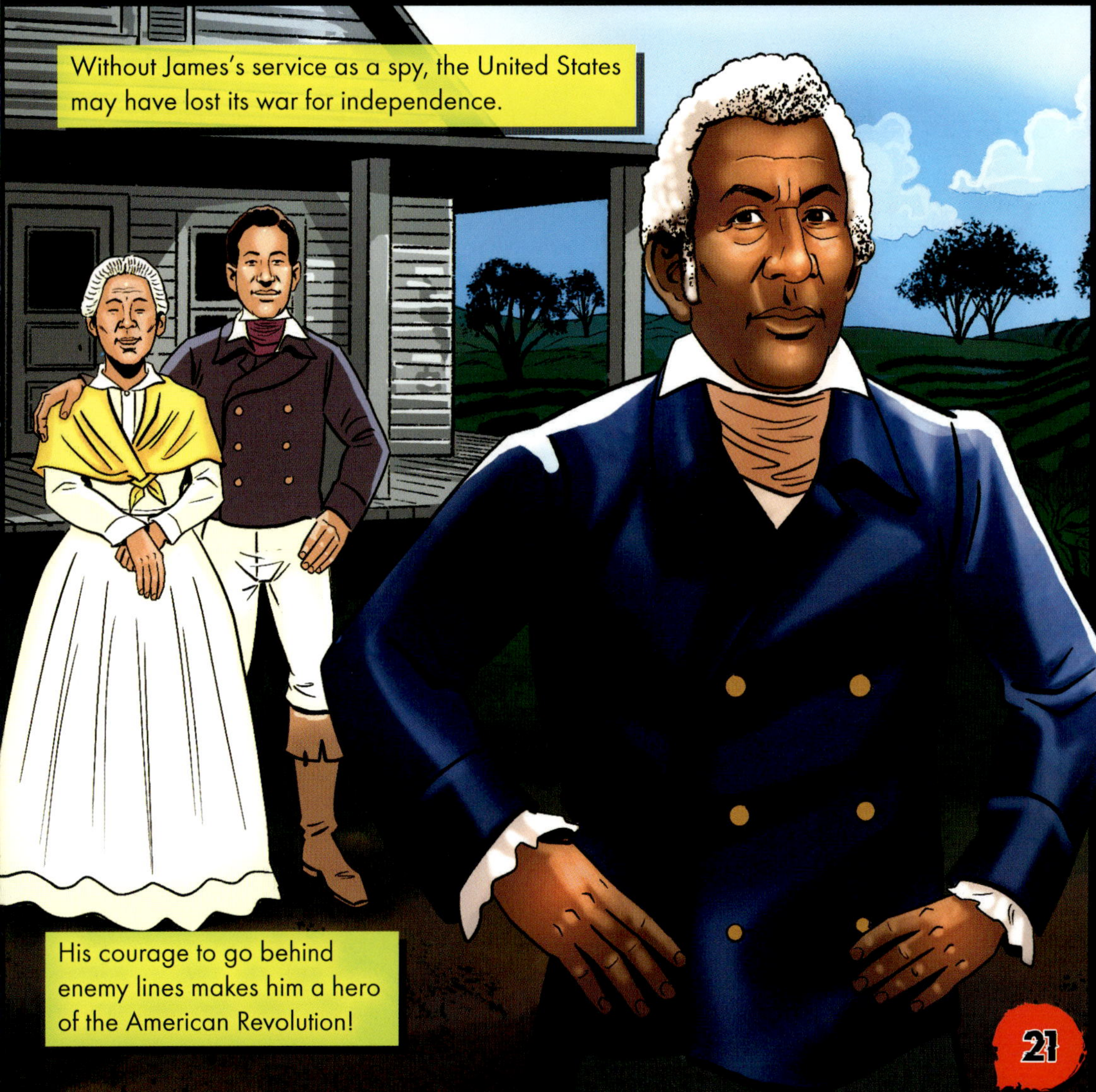
Without James's service as a spy, the United States may have lost its war for independence.
His courage to go behind enemy lines makes him a hero of the American Revolution!

MORE ABOUT JAMES LAFAYETTE

- No one is sure when James was born. Some sources believe it was around 1748. Others believe it was around 1760.

- The U.S. government promised money to people who served in the war. But they did not give money to James. He was again forced to petition Congress. He finally got the money in 1819.

- James likely died in the 1830s.

JAMES LAFAYETTE TIMELINE

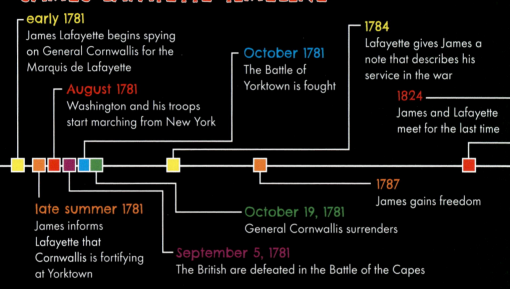

early 1781 — James Lafayette begins spying on General Cornwallis for the Marquis de Lafayette

August 1781 — Washington and his troops start marching from New York

late summer 1781 — James informs Lafayette that Cornwallis is fortifying at Yorktown

September 5, 1781 — The British are defeated in the Battle of the Capes

October 1781 — The Battle of Yorktown is fought

October 19, 1781 — General Cornwallis surrenders

1784 — Lafayette gives James a note that describes his service in the war

1787 — James gains freedom

1824 — James and Lafayette meet for the last time

JAMES LAFAYETTE MAP

- Richmond, Virginia
- Williamsburg, Virginia
- Yorktown, Virginia

GLOSSARY

admiral—a naval officer of high rank

betraying—going against one's word by helping an enemy

colonists—people who settle new land for their home country

Continental Army—the army of the 13 colonies during the American Revolutionary War

double agent—a spy who pretends to spy for one person or group while actually spying for their enemy

entrenching—putting something in a strong defensive position

fleet—a group of ships that sail together

forage—to search for food

fortified—made something strong

manservant—a male who acts as a personal servant for someone

marquis—a nobleman of high rank

patriots—colonists during the American Revolutionary War who were against British rule

petition—a formal request for something

plantation—a large farm that grows coffee beans, cotton, rubber, or other crops; plantations are mainly found in warm climates.

retreat—to withdraw

sabotage—to ruin something

slavery—the practice of forcing people to work for no pay and considering them property

strategy—a plan of action

surrenders—agrees to stop fighting

treaty—a formal agreement between two countries

trench—a long, narrow ditch

TO LEARN MORE

AT THE LIBRARY

Lowe, Mifflin. *Forgotten Founders*. Fresno, Calif.: Bushel & Peck Books, 2022.

Moening, Kate. *The American Revolutionary War*. Minneapolis, Minn.: Bellwether Media, 2024.

Rockwell, Anne. *A Spy Called James: The True Story of James Lafayette, Revolutionary War Double Agent*. Minneapolis, Minn.: Carolrhoda Books, 2016.

ON THE WEB

Factsurfer.com gives you a safe, fun way to find more information.

1. Go to www.factsurfer.com.
2. Enter "James Lafayette" into the search box and click 🔍.
3. Select your book cover to see a list of related content.

INDEX

Armistead, William, 4, 5, 6, 18, 19
Arnold, Benedict, 6, 7, 8, 9
battles, 12, 16, 17, 18
British Army, 5, 6, 7, 8, 9, 10, 11, 12, 13, 15, 16, 17
Chesapeake Bay, 16
Comte de Grasse, 15, 16
Continental Army, 4, 5, 6, 11, 12, 14, 17, 18
Cornwallis, Charles, 6, 9, 10, 12, 13, 14, 15, 16, 17

Great Britain, 4, 6, 18
historical quotes, 14
Marquis de Lafayette, 4, 5, 6, 8, 9, 10, 12, 13, 14, 15, 17, 19, 20, 21
Revolutionary War, 15, 21
Treaty of Paris, 18
United States, 18, 19, 20, 21
Virginia, 4, 7, 13, 15, 17, 18, 19, 20
Washington, George, 14, 15, 16, 17
Yorktown, Virginia, 13, 14, 15, 17, 18, 19, 20